B. Wistar Morris

Presbyterian, Baptist and Methodist testimony to confirmation, as a primitive and apostolic rite

B. Wistar Morris

Presbyterian, Baptist and Methodist testimony to confirmation, as a primitive and apostolic rite

ISBN/EAN: 9783337628208

Printed in Europe, USA, Canada, Australia, Japan

Cover: Foto ©ninafisch / pixelio.de

More available books at **www.hansebooks.com**

PRESBYTERIAN,

BAPTIST AND METHODIST

TESTIMONY TO

CONFIRMATION,

AS A PRIMITIVE AND APOSTOLIC RITE.

WITNESSES:

CALVIN, BEZA, BAXTER, PISCATOR, JOHN MILTON,
WESTMINSTER DIVINES, PRESBYTERIAN GE-
NERAL ASSEMBLY, HANMER, BAPTIST CON-
FESSIONS, COMER, OSTERVALD, COLMAN,
WESLEY, ADAM CLARKE, &c., &c.

COMPILED BY

THE REV. B. WISTAR MORRIS,

ASSISTANT MINISTER OF ST. LUKE'S CHURCH, GERMANTOWN.

"THE SONS OF STRANGERS SHALL BUILD THY WALLS."

PHILADELPHIA:

BURNS & SIEG,

COR. EIGHTH AND CHESTNUT STS.

1860.

COLLINS, PRINTER.

PREFACE.

The humblest effort to restore the Unity of the Christian family, if undertaken in a spirit of "meekness and fear," ought to receive the encouragement of all good christian people. Much has been said, of late, concerning the evils of a divided Christendom, and various expedients have been adopted to restore that primitive unity, the loss of which is now every where deplored as the sorest evil the Church labours under. It is also becoming more and more manifest to calm and reflecting men, that, if we desire primitive unity, we must seek it through the restoration of *primitive institutions* and *primitive doctrines.* Modern and human expedients having so often failed, will fail again; and there seems to be a growing conviction in the minds of many men that we had better go

(3)

back to the "old paths," and walk again in the ways of our Fathers.

The compiler of the present little work is well convinced in his own mind that this is the true course, and here offers a humble help to those who seek to know what were the institutions and doctrines of "the Primitive Church in her purest days." It is the beginning of a plan which he purposes, if allowed, to carry on, in reference to several other points of Church practice and doctrine.

Confirmation, being one of the most prominent peculiarities of our Church, and one which we are so often called upon to explain and defend, is first taken up, as a fit introduction to other doctrines and practices of equal authority and antiquity. Instead of any new arguments for the scriptural authority for this rite—for its universal prevalence for the first fifteen hundred years of the Christian Church, and for its practical utility, the present effort is simply to bring together the *admissions* of distinguished men in those Christian bodies which have laid this rite aside —to give the statements of their confessions of faith—and the history of the struggles to maintain *this* primitive practice, among those, who, in so many other things, have departed from the early usages of the Church. If the authority of the Fathers of the *Primitive* Church were in view it could be produced with great ease, and the writings of Tertullian, Cyprian, Cornelius, Dionysius, Cyril, Eusebius, Optatus, Jerome, Pacian, Ambrose, Augustine, Chrysostom, and many others, will furnish the amplest testimony to the primitive and apostolic origin of Confirmation. These, however, seem to be distrusted witnesses, and passing them all by, none will be called up but those who lived in, and after, the times of the Reformation, and who were, and are, *anti-Episcopal** in regard to the ministry, and whose descendants have long ago laid aside this "ordinance of Christ," which their fathers so much approved, and in many cases strove so hard to preserve. The motive to presenting the argument in this form, is the prevalent spirit of *deference* to *authority* in all matters of religion. Boastful as

* The only exception to this is in the cases of the Waldenses and Bohemian Brethren who were Episcopal in their ministry. See page 43.

1*

is this age of its independence in religious doctrines, there never was a time when the masses of men paid more deference to authority than at the present time. But it is to the authority of the pastor or preacher of the day. It is altogether a superficial generation in questions concerning the doctrines, discipline and usages of the Church, and most men quietly receive their faith at the hands of some distinguished Doctor or Professor of their "denomination." But if men *will* defer to human authority,—if they must call some man master, let it be those who are best entitled to this deference, who were no tyros in divinity or history, and who have been in so many other things the acknowledged masters to their fathers, and to their father's fathers.

This compilation contains matter that is wholly inaccessible to those of the laity, or clergy who are remote from our large public and private libraries, and it is now presented in this brief and portable form, hoping it may be of practical usefulness in the work of extending and building up the Church. It is hoped that in the hands of our clergy,—missionaries and others—where the Church is new and unknown, and all her *peculiarities* regarded with disfavor, this little tract may serve to soften prejudice, and lead men to the calm and dispassionate examination of her claims ; that through the faithful reception of this "Apostolic rite" they may receive the "best gifts" and be guided into the "more excellent way."

If it is found to be of any such use, the author will be encouraged to go on in his plan, with other subjects, such as an Apostolic Ministry, Episcopacy, Liturgies, &c., and to show that, before men's passions and prejudices were enlisted in the controversy, it was almost, if not quite, *universally* acknowledged that all these were part and parcel of the Primitive and Apostolic Church ; while a ministry, not Apostolic in its origin, or Episcopal in its form, was confessed by those who held it, to be a departure from primitive usage and only defensible on the ground of urgent necessity. Much material of this kind is already in hand, and much more remains scattered throughout the theological literature of an early day, which time and industry can alone collect and arrange. If, by these or any other means, the severed families of Christ's people can be brought to reverence what Melancthon called "simple and sincere antiquity," a great point will be gained. We shall then be so near the only source of truth that, "in the bright beams of its light," we may "see eye to eye," and so walk that we shall all be *one* in Christ Jesus.

CALVIN

AND THE

FRENCH AND GERMAN PROTESTANT DIVINES.

CALVIN.

———◄●►———

CONFIRMATION, OR LAYING ON OF HANDS, which is declared by the Church to be practiced "after the example of the holy Apostles," though a peculiarity in many parts of this country, was the uniform custom of the Church of Christ for the first fifteen hundred years, and is now continued, with some variety in the manner of administering, it by more than *nineteen-twentieths* of the Christian world. This alone would present to many minds an unanswerable argument in favor of its authority and utility. It will seem incredible, to not a few, that the Romish Church, the Greek Church, the Church of Sweden, the Lutheran Church, the German Reformed Church, the Waldenses, the Bohemians, the Moravians, the Church of England, the Protestant Episcopal Church in

(11)

America, the Mennonists, the Six-principle Baptists, and many others, should *all* have received and continued a practice which is without authority in the word of God, and without utility in the Church. But in addition to this weight of authority in this agreement of such a vast proportion of the Christian world, there is the additional testimony of those religious bodies and those prominent and leading divines, in whose systems this rite has no place. To give these *admissions* is the purpose of the present pages. We shall begin with the celebrated CALVIN, who deservedly stands at the head of all Presbyterian divines.

Although this distinguished Reformer rejected this rite from his system, he did not hesitate to express his belief in its primitive and *apostolic* origin. We give two extracts from his writings touching this subject. In the first of these, written in 1536, while he so heartily approves of Confirmation, and declares its antiquity, he yet questions its *apostolicity*. In the second, which was written in 1549, *thirteen* years later, he admits that the origin of this ceremony flowed from the Apostles. In his Institutes, Book 4, ch. xix, Calvin thus writes:

"It was an ancient custom in the church for the children of Christians, after they were come to the years of discretion, to be presented to the Bishop in order to fulfill that duty which was required of adults who offered themselves to baptism. For such persons were placed among the catechumens, till, being duly instructed in the mysteries of Christianity, they were enabled to make a confession of their faith before the Bishop and all the people. Therefore, those who had been baptized in their infancy, because they had not then made such a confession before the church, at the close of childhood, or the beginning of adolescence, were again presented by their parents, and were examined by the Bishop, according to the form of the catechism which was then in common use. That this exercise which deserved to be regarded as sacred and solemn, might have the greater dignity and reverence, they also practised the ceremony of the *imposition of hands.* Thus the youth, after having given satisfaction respecting his faith, was dismissed with a solemn benediction. *This custom is frequently mentioned by the ancient writers.* . . . . And though I confess that Jerome is not altogether correct in stating it to have been a custom of the *Apostles;* yet he is very

2

far from the absurdities now maintained by the Romanists. Such an imposition of hands, therefore, as is simply connected with benediction, I highly approve, and *wish it were now restored to its primitive use, uncorrupted by superstition.*"

After arguing at large, and with great earnestness, against the invention of Rome which makes Confirmation a *Sacrament*, and against the "preposterous mimicry" of the chrism, Calvin says in conclusion of this chapter—

"I sincerely wish we retained the custom, which I have stated was practised among the ancients before this abortive image of a sacrament made its appearance. For it was not *such* a confirmation as the Romanists pretend, which cannot be mentioned without injury to baptism; but catechetical exercise, in which children or youths used to deliver an account of their faith, in the presence of the church. Now it would be the best mode of catechetical instruction, if a formulary were written for this purpose, containing and stating, in a familiar manner, all the articles of our religion, in which the universal church of believers ought to agree, without any controversy. A boy of ten years of age might present himself to make a confession of his faith; he might be questioned on all the articles, and might give suitable answers: if he were ignorant of any, or did not fully understand them, he should be taught. Thus the church would witness his profession of the only true and pure faith, in which all the community of believers unanimously worship the one God. If this discipline were observed in the present day, it would certainly sharpen the inactivity of some parents, who carelessly neglect the instruction of their children as a thing in which they have no concern; but which, in that case, they could not neglect without public disgrace; there would be more harmony of faith among Christian people, nor would many betray such ignorance and want of information; some would not be so easily carried away with novel and strange tenets; in short, all would have a regular acquaintance with Christian doctrine."—Institutes, Book 4, ch. xix. sec. 13.

Taken in connection with what has been given above, where he says that this "catechetical exercise" was connected with the "ceremony of the laying on of the hands," this is as complete a description of the "Order of Confirmation," as now practised in the Episcopal Church, as if Calvin had prepared that form to suit his own ideas. Calvin's more mature views on the *origin* of this rite are found in his Commentary on the Epistle to the Hebrews, written after thirteen years of additional study of the Scriptures and the history of the Christian Church.

The first two verses of the 6th cap. of this Epistle has always been claimed as apostolic authority for Confirmation, as now practiced in the Church. In his Commentary on this passage, Calvin says:

"The Apostle here joins the imposition, or the laying on of hands with baptism, because, as there were two orders of catechumens, therefore the ceremony was two-fold. For those who were without, were not admitted to baptism until they had delivered their confession of faith. In these, therefore, catechising went before baptism. But the children of believers, since they were adopted from the womb, and belonged to the body of the church, by right of promise, were baptized while infants; and when the season of infancy had passed away, and they had been instructed in the faith, they also offered themselves to be catechised; which catechising in their case was subsequent to baptism. But then another rite was applied to them: namely, the laying on of hands.

This one passage (Hebrews vi. 2) abundantly proves *that the origin of this ceremony flowed from the Apostles*; although it was afterward turned into superstition, as the world almost always degenerates from the best institutions into corruptions."—*Commentary on Hebrews, chap.* vi.

BEZA.

THEODORE BEZA was Calvin's successor in the government of the Church in Geneva. He was a violent opponent of the errors of Romanism, and in his denunciations of the Bishops *then ruling in the church* he is thought by some to have opposed himself to the *Episcopal Office*, but the very opposite of this can be shown. He says himself: "In all which I have written against the Romish hierarchy, I have not even alluded to the polity of the Anglican Church, which to impugn, or even to notice, was not in my thoughts." And again: "If there be any— which, however, you will not easily induce me to believe—who reject the whole order

2*

of Episcopacy, God forbid that any man in his senses should assent to their madness."

Of Confirmation, he says, in his observations on Hebrews vi.—"The Apostle numbers up five heads of catechism, viz., the profession of amendment of life (*i. e.* repentance from dead works), the sum of faith concerning God, the compendious explication of doctrine that was wont to be delivered to the unlearned, especially at baptism, and the imposition of hands (when they met together to baptize infants or adult persons, and also when they came together to impose hands upon any:) the head of the resurrection of the dead, and of the future judgment." In his shorter *notes* he calls them "the heads of catechism, which contain, indeed, the chief matters of all evangelical doctrine, but were delivered in few words, and summarily, to the unlearned, viz., the profession of repentance and faith toward God. The articles of which doctrine, as they are called, were indeed required of those without the Church, at the appointed days of baptism, but from the children of all the faithful, baptized in their infancy, *when hands were laid upon them.* Among which articles, two here are expressly reckoned up, namely, the resurrection of the flesh and eternal judgment."—*Camfield on Confirmation, London,* 1682, p. 25.

It is not all-surprising that with these

views on the part of Calvin and Beza, Confirmation should again be restored to its place in the church of their founding. This was done, and an office provided for its administration. In the French Protestant (Calvinistic) Church, there is a liturgy of baptism and confirmation, which, revised, is now used in the French Protestant Church in Charleston, S. C. On page 24 may be found the Manner of receiving Catechumens, by the Confirmation of the Baptismal Vow, to a participation of the Lord's Supper.— *Quintard on Confirmation.*

FREDERIC OSTERVALD.

FREDERIC OSTERVALD was a distinguished Swiss Presbyterian divine, who studied theology at Paris and Geneva, and was afterwards appointed pastor of Neufchâtel, his native town,—a position which he adorned by his learning and zeal during a long life. He did much to revive the cause of religion in Switzerland, and, in addition to the active

duties of a pastor and preacher, found leisure
to extend his reputation as a man of learning
and piety in various able and popular works.
These works attained a great reputation
among the French protestants, by whom he
was long called " *le Grand Ostervald.*" IIis
writings were also translated into English
and German, and "Ostervald's Bible" was
long well known and much prized in England.
One very popular work of his is called " A
Treatise concerning the Causes of the Present
Corruption of Christianity." One chapter of
this work is on *Education,* in which the author
speaks as follows concerning *Confirmation :*

"Above all, it is requisite that church-men
should have a strict inspection over schools
and families, and that catechisings be more
frequent than they are. Young people ought
to be the chief objects of the care of the
pastors; no part of their office is more useful,
or rewards their labors with better success
than that. Their endeavors to mend those
who are come to age, are for the most part to
little purpose; but what they do for children
is of great benefit. If therefore they have a
zeal for the glory of God, and if they wish to
see a change in the face of the church, let
them apply themselves to the instructing of

youth, and make it their business to form a
new generation. Among the particular es-
tablishments which might be made for the
edification of the church, and the benefit of
.young people, there is one which would be
of great use, and which seems to be absolutely
necessary. And that is, with relation to
children who have attained the age of discretion, the same order should be observed
for their admission to the sacraments which
was practised in the primitive church when
catechumens were to be received into the
Church by baptism. This admission was
very solemn. A long probation went before
it. The catechumens were required to give
an account of their faith, and they bound
themselves by solemn promises and vows to
renounce the world and to live holy. No
such thing is done at this day, at the administration of baptism, because young children
are baptized; but what is not done at the
time of Baptism should be done when they
come to years of discretion. *And truly, if
there be not a public and solemn profession, a
promise in due form on the children's part, I do
not see how we can well answer what is objected
by some against infant baptism*, which yet is
a good and laudable practice. When children
are baptized they know nothing of what is
done to them; it is therefore *absolutely necessary* that when they come to the years of

reason, they should ratify and confirm the
engagements they came under by their baptism, and that they should become members
of the Church, out of knowledge and choice.
Now, the fittest time for such a confirmation
and promise, is when they are admitted to a
participation of the Holy Sacrament. The
order, then, which I mean, is this: first, that
when children desire to be admitted to the
sacrament, they should be instructed for
some weeks before, and that at the same
time they should be informed of the sacred-
ness and importance of this action, and of
the promise they are to make. In the next
place, that they should be examined, and
that they should publicly render an account
of their faith; this examination being over,
that they should be required to renew and
confirm, in a public and solemn manner,
their baptismal vow to renounce the devil
and his works, the world and the pomp of
it, the flesh and its lusts, and to promise that
they will live and die in the Christian faith,
and that then they should be admitted to the
communion by benediction and prayers. It
will, no doubt, seem to some that I am here
proposing a novelty, and that, too, not very
necessary; that there is no occasion for all
this solemnity; that it is enough to examine
and exhort children in private, and that this
confirmation of the baptismal vow is included

and supposed in the admission to the sacrament. To this I say, that the order I propose will be thought a novelty *by none but such as do not know what was anciently practised,* and who call innovation, every thing which does not agree with the custom of their country or their church. This is an *imitation of the ancient and the apostolic order,* and besides, this establishment being altogether suitable to the nature of the Christian religion, as I have just now made it appear, it ought not to be rejected.

As for what is said, that it is sufficient if children are examined and admitted in private; I answer, that the corruption of the age we live in is so great that, in many churches, this admission, and the examination which precedes it, is but three or four hours' work, and sometimes less. Pastors, and those to whom this function is committed, do often go about it very negligently; they content themselves with some questions which, for the most part, relate only to doctrine and controversy; they address to children, general exhortations to piety, but they take no care to instruct them in morals, or to examine their conduct; they do not require of them an express ratification of the baptismal vow. I know there are pastors who do their duty, but the best thing would be, to have this form of examination and admission regulated in such a manner that it might not be in the breast of every minister to do in this matter as he thinks fit. And that all this might be done the more orderly; it would be fitting, that, *according to the practice of the Primitive Church,* some persons should be appointed on purpose to instruct young people and catechumens. What care soever may be taken of children, and whatever may be done for them in private instructions, it is certain *that public and solemn exhortations* on the one hand, and *promises on the other,* would make a much greater impression upon them. They would then look upon their admission with respect, they would remember it all their lives, and this solemnity would prove as useful and edifying to the whole church, as it would be to the young people. I offer this with the greater confidence, because an order like this has been settled of late in some churches, and is there observed with extraordinary success." *Ostervald's Corruptions &c.— Watson's Theological Tracts*—Cambridge Edition, 1785, vol. vi. pp. 277, 278.

PISCATOR.

John Piscator was a German Divine of great celebrity in the latter part of the sixteenth and beginning of the seventeenth century. He embraced the doctrines of Calvin, and was made Professor of Divinity and sacred literature in the University of Herborn, in 1584. His learning and ability was held in such estimation that students crowded to his lectures from France, Hungary, Poland, and the northern kingdoms of Europe. He died in 1626, leaving a commentary in Latin upon all the books of the Old and New Testament, beside many voluminous, practical and controversial treatises.

On the text, Hebrews, vi. 1–2, he says:'

"This doctrine (of repentance from dead works, and faith towards God) was wont to be delivered to the Catechumens before they were baptized, or *confirmed in the christian faith by the imposition of hands,* although we think this imposition of hands to be a matter of free observance, as having, indeed, *Apostolic example,* but not a precept from Christ. At first sight there seems to be six heads of doctrine distinctly reckoned up; but if one shall more accurately weigh them, they may be referred to four, or to three; for the third and fourth, viz., Baptism and impositions of hands seem not here to be propounded as peculiar heads of doctrine, but put among the rest to declare the *circumstances of time* wherein

3

these *fundamentals were wont to be propounded unto beginners, namely, at that time, when the adults were admitted unto baptism, and also when those who were baptized in their infancy, and afterwards instructed in their childhood, were wont by the church to be confirmed in the christian faith by the imposition of hands."—Camfield, &c., p. 26.*

RIVET.

ANDREW RIVET was a French Calvinistic Divine, of great piety, learning, and eminence. In 1620 he was appointed Professor of Divinity at Leyden, where he remained till his death in 1647. He left several theological works, as well as an entire commentary on the Scriptures. Of Confirmation he thus speaks:

"The imposition of hands joined with the doctrine of baptism, Heb. vi. 2, refers to that solemn benediction of baptized persons which the ancients so often speak of, and which was in use in the Primitive Church, which was, that when children, who were baptized in infancy, could give an account of their faith to the satisfaction of the Pastor, he then laid his hands upon them and blessed them, commending them to God, and thereby confirming them in the profession of the christian religion." This custom having been corrupted among the Papists, he says: " *They* had restored to its lawful use by catechising, instruction, and benediction of children in prayer before they were admitted to the Lord's Supper."—*Rivet, Cathol. Orth. Tract* iii. 29, quoted in Bingham, vol. 8, p. 173.

He says again, in another place, in addition to much the same language as the above:

"If they of the Church of Rome would be content with this prayer and commendation of adult persons to God, after a solemn examination, we should willingly acquiesce therein ; if they would demand no more than that rite which *Calvin wished to have restored, and which, for the substance of it, is now religiously observed in our churches.*"—*Synops. Pur. Theo. Disp.* 47. p. 13, quoted by Bingham, vol. 8, p. 173.

HERZOG.

Under the article " *Confirmation,*" in Herzog's Protestant Theological Encyclopedia,

is the following: "In the Apostolic Church
the laying on of hands was connected with
baptism, as the means of communicating the
gift of the Holy Ghost. . . . . . Baptism was
incomplete without the laying on of hands,
and the gift of the Holy Ghost: wherefore,
Protestant polemics should never have allowed
itself to accept the declaration, that these
passages (Acts xix. 6; viii. 12–19. Heb.
vi. 1–2, &c.) did not refer to the Holy Ghost.
but only to the special gifts of the Spirit in
Apostolic times." In speaking of the views
of the Reformers in reference to this rite
the article further says: "Confirmation was
rejected as a *sacrament* by the Protestants
from the beginning, for the two-fold reason,
that it lacked the sign of a sacrament, and
detracted from baptism. It was practised in
Pomerania, Geneva, &c., though everywhere
divested of a *Sacramental* character. The in-
tercessory laying on of hands takes the place
of the anointing with oil, and the act itself
is regarded as a confession of faith. A
difference in the procedure between the Lutherans and Reformed scarcely existed. . . . . .
The ceremony did not, however, extend itself
further toward the end of the 17th century
but even went out of use where it existed,
with but a few exceptions. Its continuance
was preserved by pietism. After several attempts (as by Henisius, in Frankfort on the

Oder,) Spencer re-established it in Frankfort on the Maine, in 1666. Its re-introduction into the Protestant Church was now so rapid that it seemed as if a universal desire existed for it. Several Churches introduced it, the Government approved, and then law made it binding; this was in general the way it spread. Still it required the whole of the past and part of the present century to make its re-introduction general; and it was not done everywhere without opposition."

3*

ENGLISH PRESBYTERIANS AND NON-CONFORMISTS.

"ASSEMBLY'S ANNOTATIONS."

THIS is the title of a Commentary on the Scriptures, of high origin and authority among the Presbyterians. It was written by a Committee appointed by the Presbyterian Parliament in 1648–9, composed chiefly of those who were Members of the Westminster Assembly, whence it has always been known as the "Assembly's Annotations." The names of this Committee are given by Neal in his history of the Puritans, vol. 3., p. 386, and we find among them those of high distinction for learning and ability.

On Hebrews vi. 2, is the following comment:

["Laying, &c.,] which is usually called confirmation, which stood first in examining those who had been baptized, what progress they had made in the doctrine of Christianity. Secondly, in praying for them, that God would continue them in the faith, and give them more grace, strengthening them by his Holy Spirit. Now when the chief Pastor or Pastors of the church prayed for them, they laid their hands upon them, whence the apostolical constitution was called the laying on of hands. So Augustine, and so most of the fathers, with one consent. Or understand thereby a ceremony used in the ordination of ministers."

On Acts xix. 5, the Annotations say:

"Not that Paul did re-baptize them. These words relate not unto the words of Paul, but unto their hearing of John's doctrine: and therefore Paul is not said to have baptized them, but to have laid his hands upon them: that is, a posture and action of confirmation, not initiation. Baptism is a new birth of the whole man: as we can be born but once in the flesh, so we can be born but once in the spirit."

[v. 6. Laid his hands upon them,] chap. vi. 6, and viii. 17, he laid his hands upon them for confirmation; we read not that he re-baptized them.

DR. GOUGE.

DR. WILLIAM GOUGE was a celebrated Puritan Minister, a member of the Westminster Assembly, who took an active part in the various proceedings instituted, by the then ruling powers, for the reformation of the Church. He was one of the Committee appointed by Parliament to prepare the Commentary on the Scriptures, known as the "Assembly's Annotations," to which reference is made above. His principal work is a Commentary on the Epistle to the Hebrews, where, under the first and second verses of chapter sixth, he says :

" Ordinary cases wherein *imposition of hands* was used, were—1. Blessing children by our Saviour. 2. Setting men apart to the public function of ministers of the Word. 3. Deputing men to some special work. 4. Confirming such as had been instructed in the principles of religion. This last particular (meaning confirmation) he says " is not *expressly* set down in Scripture, but gathered out of it by the Ancient Orthodox Fathers, and with a joint consent afterwards by most divines, not Papists only, but Protestants also."—*Camfield*, p. 35.

CALAMY.

EDMUND CALAMY was a distinguished English Presbyterian Minister, who wrote and preached much in favor of the Presbyterian form of Church Government, and had a share in drawing up the celebrated vindication of that form published in London in 1650, and also the Jus Divinum in 1654. He was engaged with Hoadly, Bishop of Winchester, in a controversy on Non-Conformity. He published in 1704, a "Practical Discourse concerning Vows, with a special reference to Baptism and the Lord's Supper," from which the following is an extract:

"And here it may be inquired, whether or no it be fitting, requisite, or allowable, that imposition of hands, joined with serious prayers to God for the strengthening and confirming grace of his Spirit, for those who come to own their *baptismal vows* openly in the face of a Christian congregation; and an authoritative benediction on the part of the minister, as God's officer, should be used on this occasion?" "Whereto I answer, that there is a general unanimity among those who have been most diligent in searching into ecclesiastical antiquity, in reporting this as the current practice of the primitive Church; and that not only while miraculous gifts continued, but afterward. That it is convenient and warrantable by Scripture as well as antiquity, was the opinion of our first reformers here in England, and the most celebrated divines we have had amongst us ever since. This was also the judgment of the learned Grotius, who was perhaps one of the greatest men these parts of the world ever produced. Nay, the same was the sentiment of the famous Calvin, who founded confirmation by imposition of hands on Heb. vi. 2, where we find *laying on of hands* in the rank of fundamentals, in the fourth place, after repentance, faith, and baptism, and before the resurrection and eternal judgment. On which passage of Scripture, Calvin hath this note: '*That this one place sufficiently manifests that the ceremony of laying on of hands on those who passed out of the infant into the adult state of believers, upon their open professing the Christian faith, had its rise from the Apostles ;*' and therefore he declares that, '*though the Romanists had superstitiously abused it, yet he was altogether against laying it aside, but for keeping the institution pure.*' The same was Beza's judgment. Herein also *Gerrard* agrees with divers of the most famous Lutheran divines. And finally, that eminent servant of God, Mr. Richard Baxter (than whom this nation never afforded one more earnestly intent on the promoting practical godliness or true Christian discipline) hath wrote a treatise on purpose for the revival of this antiquated practice, which is entitled, ' *Confirmation and Restoration the Necessary Means of Reformation and Reconciliation*;' whereto I refer those that would desire full satisfaction in this matter." He continues: "However, I shall take this opportunity of warning all to take heed of imagining that every thing is to be quite laid aside that hath been abused to superstition. That's a very fond conceit, and some that have unwarily imbibed it, little observed whither it would lead if pursued with rigor. Suppose a man superstitiously abuses the Scripture, (which I am satisfied is no impossible thing,) am I therefore obliged to lay it aside as useless? What an unhappy case were I in, if another man's superstition might rob me of that which would be so useful to me! Any one almost would be ready in such a case to say, what an argument is another's abuse against my right use of that invaluable book which God hath left as a legacy to His Church? In like manner, how weak an argument is it for persons to say the Papists have abused Confirmation, or they have abused absolution, to superstition, therefore we must lay it aside! What, I pray, hinders us from using that rightly which they have abused? We need not throw away the wheat that we may get rid of the chaff, for the fan will suffice to separate and scatter that, and leave the wheat remaining."

MILTON.

The celebrated Puritan, JOHN MILTON, Secretary to Cromwell, says in his work on *Christian Doctrine*: "Confirmation or imposition of hands, was, it is true, administered by Christ; not, however, as a sacrament, but as a form of blessing, according to a common Jewish custom, derived, probably from patriarchal times, when fathers were accustomed to lay their hands on their children in blessing them, and magistrates on those whom they appointed their successors, as Moses on Joshua. Hence the Apostles usually laid their hands on such as were baptized or chosen to any ecclesiastical office: *usually*, I say, not always, for, though we read of imposition of hands on the seven deacons, we do not find that this ceremony was practised towards Matthias when he was numbered with the eleven Apostles.*   In the case of the baptized, imposition of hands conferred, not indeed saving grace, but miraculous powers and the extraordinary gifts of the Spirit. Hence, although the Church rejects this ceremony *as a Sacrament, she retains it with great propriety and advantage as a symbol of blessing,* Heb. vi. 2. *The doctrine of baptisms, and of laying on of hands.*"—*Milton on Christian Doctrine*, p. 449. Edit. Cambridge, 1825.

HANMER.

JONATHAN HANMER who was a distinguished non-conformist divine of the middle of the 17th century wrote a work in favor of *Confirmation* entitled "An Exercitation upon Confirmation—the Ancient Way of completing Church Membership," which was published in London in 1658. The preface to this work was written by Richard Baxter, who says that Mr. Hanmer wrote "very learnedly and piously, endeavoring the restoration

* There is no proof that it was *not* done, and moreover, if this makes against anything, it is against the practice of laying on hands in *ordination!*

4

of this practice." The occasion of this production is of great interest, being the agreement of the associated non-conformist ministers, in the county in which Mr. Baxter was settled, to adopt some ceremony for the "solemn transition of infants into church membership." Baxter says in the preface to his own work on Confirmation,—

"When the book of Mr. Hanmer was read, the design was generally approved (as far as I can learn), and very acceptable to men of all parties. But many of them called to me to try whether some more Scripture proofs might not be brought for it, and at the desire of some Reverend Godly brethren I hastily drew up this which is here offered you."

BAXTER.

The celebrated non-conformist minister, Richard Baxter, who so earnestly opposed the Church of England, came in time to regard the rite of *Confirmation* with great favor, and to confess that its want was "the greatest corruption of the Church of any outward thing he remembered." With this conviction he set about the work referred to above. It is a very long and elaborate production, and discusses the subject in every possible view, till it is thoroughly exhausted. In a little work like this, we can of course give but brief extracts. It is entitled, " Confirmation and Restoration the necessary means of Reformation and Reconciliation." We quote from the London folio edition of Baxter's Works, 1707, 4th volume, p. 254. The author states, that the chief object he had in writing on *Confirmation*, was to satisfy his own earnest desires after the reformation and reconciliation of the churches; to which, he adds, " I do very confidently apprehend this excellent work, (the Restoring of Confirmation) to have a singular tendency."

Under the head of the 13th *Proposition*, entitled " *Ministerial* Imposition of Hands in Confirmation," etc., Mr. Baxter says:—" For the first of the proposition I think it may suffice—1. That imposition of hands was used in Scripture times; and so used, as may invite us to imitation, but not deter us from it at all. 2. And that it hath been since of ordinary use in the Universal Church, in this very case, so that *no other original can be found* but Apostolical; yea, we *have exceeding probable evidence, that the use of it was never interrupted from the days of the Apostles down to the Reformation.* 3. Nor is it laid aside in many of the Reformed Churches. So that you will find that as it is easy to prove *lawful, so it is more likely to be a Divine Institution,* necessary, *necessitate præcepti,* than to be *unlawful.*"—p. 268.

Under this same *Proposition,* we find the following in reference to the *ceremony of laying on hands,*—" But let us inquire whether the Scriptures lay not some kind of obligation on us to use this ceremony in Confirmation, to which end let these several things be considered. 1. *We find in Scripture a blessing of church members with laying on of hands.* 2. *We find in Scripture that the Holy Ghost is promised in a special manner to believers, over and above that measure of the Spirit which caused them to believe.* 3. *We find that Prayer with Laying on of Hands, was the outward means to be used by Christ's ministers for the procuring of this blessing.* 4. *We find that this was a fixed ordinance to the church, and not a temporary thing.*" Ib., p. 271. Under this 4th Proposition concerning the *continuance* of Confirmation in the Church, Baxter says:

"When I have proved it once *appointed*, it lieth on the contrary-minded to prove it changed or ceased. If I show them an obligation once laid, they must prove it taken off. Their only argument is, that the persons and occasions were only extraordinary, and are ceased, and therefore so is the sign and means. To which I answer—1. By denying the antecedent; both as to persons and occasions. They were not *only extraordinary*. 2. By denying the consequence as it is inferred from the persons. For extraordinary *persons* were our patterns for *ordinary durable work*. But I prove the negative. The use and ends of the ancient Imposition of hands do still continue: Therefore, we are to judge that the sign and means is not to cease. The baptized believer may still want the joy of the Holy Ghost, and boldness of access to God, and the shedding abroad of fuller love in the heart. Now to have a messenger of Christ that hath received a binding and loosing power, in the name of Christ to encourage us in our profession, and to put up solemn prayers for us, and as it were to take us by the hand and place us in the higher form, and make particular application of the promise to us, and bless us in the name of Christ, by virtue of their ministerial office, this must needs tend much to confirm, and comfort, and en-

courage the weak. The Scripture signifieth
to us, that imposition of hands was of standing use in the Church, and therefore not to
cease with miracles. In Heb. vi. 2, we find
it named among the parts of the *foundation*,
Laying on of Hands. .... The last thing
I have to do is to argue from the practice of
the Church. If the Universal Church of
Christ have used Confirmation by Prayer
and Laying on of Hands, as a practice received from the Apostles,—and no other beginning of it can be found;—then have we
no reason to think the ceremony to be
ceased. But the antecedent is true, as I come
now briefly to prove, supposing what Mr.
Hanmer hath said. It is commonly known
that the ancientest Canons of the *Church
do speak of this as the unquestioned practice and
duty* of the Church; so that to recite Canons were loss of time in so known a
case."—*Ib.* 272.

Mr. Baxter then gives the testimony of the
Fathers to the antiquity of Confirmation,
quoting from Ignatius, Tertullian, Cyprian,
&c. Much more is said by this distinguished
and learned Non-conformist on this subject
—these quotations, however, are sufficient
to show of what sacred origin and utility he
considered this rite.

WALDENSES AND BOHEMIANS.

WALDENSES.

THE chief purpose of this work being to collect the testimony of *Non-Episcopal* authorities, that of the *early Waldenses* would of course not be included, if this purpose was strictly adhered to. But there are such vague and erroneous notions prevalent concerning these early Reformers in the Church, that we shall give their testimony on the subject of *Confirmation*, as if they *had* laid aside this and other primitive and apostolic usages of the Church. As for Episcopacy, it is capable of the clearest proof, that for a long while they carefully maintained this form of the ministry.* When the Bohemian Brethren, who

---

* In keeping with our purpose of giving the testimony of Non-Episcopalians, we subjoin here the testimony of Dr. J. P. Wilson, former Pastor of the *First Presbyterian Church in Philadelphia*, in reference to the *Episcopacy* of the Waldenses. It will be found in his " Primitive Government of Christian Churches,"

had been driven by persecution into the
woods and mountains, came to fear the loss
of a lawful ministry by the death of their

published in Philadelphia, in 1833. On page 214,
where he is treating of the "Waldenses of Bohemia
and Moravia," he says—"The latter (referring to
John Huss) adopted the doctrines of Wickliffe, and
was burned in 1415, and is accounted the founder of
the Society of Unitas Fratrum. . . . These have been
also called Waldenses, from their union with those
of Austria. *These being Episcopal, there was still neither
place for, nor the existence of, lay presbyters."* Again, on
page 215, he says—"Being cut off from ordination,
both from the Roman and Greek Churches, in 1467,
the Brethren obtained *Episcopal ordination* for certain
men chosen to be *seniors,* superintendents, or bishops, from Stephen, who was the last Bishop of the
Waldenses (Vallenses) and was burned at Vienna in
1468. This *excellent evangelical, and persecuted people,*
had more respect for sound doctrines than scrupu-
lous correctness in matters of church government,
Their prejudices have always been for the Episcopal
government, even whilst groaning under the oppres-
sions of diocesan Episcopacy. From the commence-
ment of their new episcopate, which was about fifty
years before the Reformation, they had eight kinds
of officers—*elders, almoners, inspectors* of buildings,
ministers, acoluths (candidates for the ministry, who
read homilies) *deacons* who preach ; *presbyters* or *priests,*
who administer ordinances ; and *bishops,* whom they
denominate *seniors."*

This "*prejudice"* on the part of this "excellent and
evangelical people" for the "Episcopal government" is not very remarkable, since they had never
known or heard of any other since the days of
the Apostles. But the author of this work, while
striving to do the best he can with stubborn *facts* of
the early history of the Church, is withal so candid
in his admissions on this point, that we can not re-

faithful Pastors that had fled thither with them, they held a Council in 1467, composed of seventy ministers out of Bohemia and Moravia, who appointed three of their number by lot, whom they sent to these *Waldenses* on the confines of Moravia and Austria, whither they too were fled for conscience' sake. There they found Stephanus the Waldensian *Bishop*, by whom they were consecrated, and sent home with Episcopal power. The full account of this may be seen in *Du-*

frain from giving the following note of his to page 215, in which he rebukes Perrin, a Waldensian of later date, for the want of the same spirit.

"Perrin says, 'At the time when the doctrine of John Huss was received and entertained there, the ministers, *elders* and Protestants of Bohemia say, &c.'"

"And again, in speaking of the Martyrdom of the Austrian Waldensian Bishop, Stephen, he calls him '*an elderly man.*' In page 19 he says, 'There was a certain man called Bartholomew, who founded and governed the churches in Bulgaria, Croatia, Dalmatia, and Hungary, and ordained ministers, &c.' Perrin *must have known* that these *elders* and clergymen were *bishops;* but writing a century after the Reformation, *he wishes to cast a veil over the government of those churches.* What confidence can be placed in such a writer?"

We commend the statements of this candid and learned Presbyterian divine to those who are perpetually referring to the *Waldenses* for the origin and model of the Presbyterian form of Church Government.

rell's Government of Reformed Churches, pp. 11 and 12.—Ed. 1662.

As to *Confirmation*, the Waldenses, in the year 1504, exhibited their Confession to Ladislaus, King of Hungary, in which they thus speak of this rite—

" We do profess, with a faith taken out of the divine Scriptures, that *in the times of the Apostles* this was observed : whoever being come to the ripeness of years, had not received the promised gifts of the Holy Ghost, received them afterward by *prayer and imposition of hands for the Confirmation of faith.* The same we think also of *infants.* Whosoever being baptized, hath come over to the true faith, which he resolves to imitate, indeed, amidst adversities and contumelies, in that manner, that a new birth and life of graces, may seem discovered in his spirit or temper. Such an one ought to be brought and set before the Bishop or Priest, when being questioned of the truth of Faith, and the divine commands, and also his own good-will, settled intentions, and works of truth ; if he shall witness, by his confession, that all these things are so, he is to be confirmed in the hope of truth already attained, and furthermore to be holpen by *the Churches' prayers, that an increase of the gifts of the Holy Ghost,* may accrue unto him for the establishment and warfare of faith. Lastly, by *imposition of hands to Confirm the promises of God* and the truth. in the power of the name of the Father, and of his Word, and of the Holy Spirit, let him be joined to the Churches' Communion."

Again in their Apology to the Marquess of Brandenburgh, in 1552, speaking of children that have been baptized, they add :

" When they shall have come to *years of discretion*, and now understand the account of their faith, and begin to love Christ in good earnest, we bring them to the profession of these things, even whatsoever they have attained to by the help of their *parents or Godfathers, or by the ministry of the Church, that they may themselves*, of their own accord, and most freely, own and profess, all these things before the whole Church, to their own salvation, in the celebration of the rite of imposition of hands; which being done, they are Confirmed. And there is forthwith given them full power and right to communicate of the Body and Blood of Christ with the faithful."—*Camfield*, p. 30.

BOHEMIAN BRETHREN.

THE BOHEMIAN BRETHREN were a body of Reformers who sprung up in Bohemia, in the year 1467. They were a remnant of the Sclavonic Church, and disciples of Wickliffe, Huss, and Jerome of Prague. They treated the Pope as Anti-Christ, and held the Scriptures to be the only rule of faith and practice, and have sometimes gone under the same name with the Waldenses. In 1504, they were accused of heresy by the Romanists to king Ladislaus, who published an edict against them, forbidding them to hold any meetings. When Luther declared himself against the Church of Rome, the Bohemian Brethren endeavored to join his party, but at first were not allowed, till 1523, when a deputation was sent to him, giving a full account of their faith. They were then acknowledged by Luther, as a society of Christians, " whose doctrines came nearest to the purity of the Gospel." They published another Confession in 1535, renouncing *anabaptism*, which they practised at first, upon which a union was concluded with the Lutherans, and afterward with the Zuinglians, whose opinions from thenceforth they continued to follow. Their last *Bishop* was Comenius, who has left an account of the manner of administering the rite of Confirmation among these early Protestants, which is so conformable to the present custom of the Church, that we give it entire. He says—

"The young ones, having been taught the heads of religion, at home by their parents and sureties, or at school by their masters, are publicly delivered to the care of their pastors in the church, before the receiving of the Lord's Supper, most usually at the time of pastoral visitation, after this manner:

1. The words of Christ, Mat. xi. 28, are read, with a short aplication of them.

2. The youth of both sexes, appointed thereunto, and pre-examined by their pastors, are placed in order in the middle of the Church.

3. They are then asked whether they will renew the covenant they entered into with God at baptism.

4. This being consented to by them, the heads of that covenant are explained according to the form prescribed by the Apostle to Titus, chap ii. 11, 12, 13. And they are commanded openly, before the Church, to renounce the world, the devil, and the flesh, &c.

5

5. Next, a profession of the faith is required of them, so that they all repeat aloud the Apostles' Creed.

6. Then, on their bended knees, saying after the minister, they pray unto God to forgive the sins of their youth, and strengthen them by his Holy Spirit, unto all the good purposes of his will; which also the whole assembly doth, praying for them: after which prayers,—

7. There is declared to these young disciples, and the whole church, absolution, and the right of the sons of God in participating in the Supper of the Lord. And lastly there is added the *Apostolic rite* of imposition of hands, with the invocation of the name of God upon them, to strengthen (or confirm) the hope of his heavenly grace."

AMERICAN PRESBYTERIANS AND CONGREGATIONALISTS.

GENERAL ASSEMBLY.

One of the most important acknowledgments of the primitive character and utility of the rite of Confirmation, is in the report of a committee, appointed by the General Assembly of the Presbyterian Church in the United States, in the year 1811, "to draught a plan for disciplining baptized children." This committee consisted of the Rev. Drs. James Richards, Samuel Miller, and John B. Romeyn, three of the most learned Presbyterian divines of that day. They submitted their report in the following year, which the Assembly ordered to be published, "recommending it to the serious consideration of all the presbyteries and ministers, that in due time a decision may be had on the important subjects discussed in the report."

The report is a learned and elaborate production, making an octavo pamphlet of over fifty pages, and refers to the writings of the fathers, and the practice of the Primitive Church, with a spirit of respect and deference that has become very rare in these latter days. On pages 13, 14, and 15, it speaks thus, of the disciplining of baptized children, and the rite of *Confirmation*.

" The Primitive Church considered herself as the common mother of all baptized children, and exercised a corresponding care over them, that they might be trained up as a generation to serve the Lord. She did not, indeed, in so many words, in her public confessions, adopted and enlarged from time to time, to meet prevailing errors, avow the principle; nor was it necessary, for the principle was recognized in the requirement of a promise or vow from the baptized person, that he would live according to the rules of Christianity. As this vow could not be made by infants, it was *required from those who presented* them. *These persons, whether parents* or *others*, besides receiving themselves, as members of the church, the seal of baptism, became responsible, not only for the instruction, but for the admonition and rebuke, if necessary, of the children baptized. Children were presented to baptism, not so much by those in whose hands they were brought (though by them too, if they were good and faithful men), as by the whole society of saints. The whole Church was their mother.* That this principle was in fact avowed by the Primitive Church in her practice, though not in words in her confession, *appears from the design of the rite of Confirmation; the attention which was paid to the instruction of baptized children,* and the discipline actually inflicted upon them in case of improper conduct. First, *it appears that a rite called Confirmation was administered by the imposition of the hand of the minister, or Bishop, or elder, together with prayer* on baptized children, at a certain age. *Both Calvin in his Institutes, and Owen in his Commentary on the Hebrews, acknowledge that this practice existed at a very early period in the Church.* The latter thus states its design. ' When they (that is the children of believers, baptized in their infancy) were established in the knowledge of these necessary truths, (of which he makes mention before), and had resolved on personal obedience to the Gospel, they were offered unto the fellowship of the faithful; and here, on giving the same account of their faith and repentance which others had done before they were baptized, they were admitted into the communion of the Church, the elders *thereof laying their hands on them in token of their acceptation, and*

* This is the institution of *Sponsors*, against which so many persons now object.

5*

praying for their Confirmation in the faith.'
This rite, which was originally confined to
those who were baptized in their infancy,
was afterward administered to adults, immediately upon their baptism. In process of
time, when the Church became grossly corrupted in her practice as well as doctrine,
it was administered to infants immediately
after baptism, that they might receive the
Lord's Supper. This historical fact, while
it exhibits a most deplorable superstition,
strikingly illustrates the design of *Confirmation*, as already stated from Dr. Owen.
'By this rite it came to pass,' saith the
judicious Hooker, 'that children in the
expectation thereof, were seasoned with the
principles of true religion, before malice and
corrupt examples depraved their minds, a
good foundation was laid betimes for direction of the course of their whole lives; the
seed of the Church of God was preserved
sincere and sound; the prelates and fathers
of God's family, to whom the care of their
souls belonged, saw by trial and examination
of them, a part of their own heavy burden
discharged, reaped comfort by beholding the
first beginnings of true godliness in tender
years, glorified him whose praise they found
in the mouth of infants, and neglected not so
fit an opportunity of giving every one fatherly
encouragement and exhortation; whereunto
imposition of hands and prayer being added,

[these italics are in the report] our warrant for the great good effect thereof, is the same which patriarchs, prophets, priests, apostles, fathers and men of God have had for such their particular invocations and benedictions, as no man, I suppose, professing truth and religion, will easily think to have been without fruit.'

This rite of Confirmation, thus administered to baptized children when arrived to competent years and previously instructed and prepared for it, with the express view of their admission to the Lord's Supper, shows clearly that the primitive Church, in her purest days, exercised the authority of a mother over her baptized children.

This Report may be seen in the library of the "Presbyterian Historical Society," in Philadelphia, to the gentlemanly librarian of which I am indebted for the use of a copy of it. The value of this Report to us is, that men of such high standing among the Presbyterians maintain it to be an historical *fact*, that the rite of Confirmation, or laying on of hands with prayer, upon persons previously baptized, was the practice of "THE PRIMITIVE CHURCH IN HER PUREST DAYS." If so, *then* we may well ask, Why not so now?

With regard to the opinion of the authors of the Report, and of Dr. Owen, that Confirmation was administered by the ministers or elders, whom they also style bishops, it may be sufficient to adduce the following from the "judicious Hooker," which occurs in the same section that contains the passage on which they bestow so much commendation.

"The cause of severing Confirmation from Baptism (for most commonly they went together) was sometimes in the minister, which being of inferior degree, might baptize but not confirm, as in their case it came to pass whom Peter and John did confirm, whereas Philip had before baptized them." Quoting from Cyprian and Jerome, the "judicious Hooker" observes: "By this it appeareth that when the *ministers* of baptism were *persons of inferior degree*, the *bishops* did after confirm whom such had before baptized." *Eccl. Pol.*, book v. sect. 66.

CONGREGATIONAL.

Although we have no positive admissions from the early Puritans concerning *Confirmation*, we still have their general endorsement of the doctrines of the Church of England, which it may not be amiss to give,

to show that they were not *opposed* to that
Church, as many of their descendants now
unfortunately are.

In the "Seven Articles," sent by the
Church of Leyden to the Council of England, in 1617, and signed by the pastor,
Robinson, and the elder, Brewster, this is
most plainly stated. The first of these articles is as follows:—

"To the Confession of Faith, published
in the name of the Church of England, and
to every article thereof we do, with the Reformed Churches where we live, and also
elsewhere, assent wholly." Article 2d says:
"As we do acknowledge the doctrine of faith
there taught, so do we the fruits and effects
of the same doctrine to the begetting of saving faith in thousands in the land, (Confor-
mists and re-Conformists,) as they are called,
with whom also as with our brethren we do desire to keep Spiritual Communion in peace, and
will practise in our parts all lawful things."
These articles may all be seen in Steele's
"Life and Times of Elder Brewster," p. 316.

Robinson says again, in his treatise on
the "Lawfulness of hearing the Ministers of
the Church of England." "For myself I
believe with my heart before God, and profess with my tongue, and have before the
world, that I have one and the same faith,

hope, spirit, baptism, and Lord which I had in the church of England, and none other." *Ibid.* p. 319.

This is worth remembering by some of the descendants of these who are now so ready to charge this Church with all manner of unscriptural doctrines.

Of *Confirmation*, Cotton Mather plainly approved in his *Ratio Disciplinæ*, p. 104.

DR. CÓLMAN.

Dr. Benjamin Colman, a Congregational minister of much learning and distinction, was the first pastor of the Brattle Street congregation, in Boston. He died about the middle of the last century, leaving numerous publications.

Among his published sermons there is one on the "Ten Virgins," the following extract, from which is published in the *Episcopal Watchman* of 1829, p. 52.

"The confession of the name of Christ is, after all, very lame, and will be so, till the discipline which Christ ordained be restored, and *the rite of Confirmation be recovered to its full use and solemnity.* The reason why the one has dwindled into a useless name is be-

cause the other is lost. *There is a discipline
which our Saviour has instituted which should
be to His Church forever a sacred and invio-
lable order.* The honor of religion and the
safety of souls call for it. The first and
grand defect in order seems to me to be the
abuse or total want of a regular recognition
of the baptismal vow, by those that have
been baptized in infancy, as they grow up.
If this were strictly attended to, so would
the exercise of a severe watch, in all likeli-
hood, continue, and the administration of
just censures would follow as occasion required. But a false step being made here,
it runs into great confusion and disorder.
Your external profession or confession of
the faith is very imperfect without a public,
serious declaration of it in the face of the
congregation, at the demand of your pastors
when you come to years of discretion. It
is not enough that you have been baptized,
and had a Christian education, and have
given your attendance on the public worship
of Christ from your infancy, but you are to
say that you stand to your Baptism—*take
that vow upon you, and confirm and ratify* all
that was done by your parents in the solemn
duty of devoting you to God. This is the
most explicit act of confessing Christ that is
done by a Christian ordinarily in his whole
life."—(See Chapman's Sermons.)

BAPTISTS.

In this body of Protestant Christians, the rite of *Confirmation*, or "laying on of hands," as they generally called it, has had a very interesting history. In one or more of its various divisions it is still practised. Such is the case with the "Seventh-day Baptists," and with the "Six-principle Baptists." In the Confession of Faith of the former of these, adopted at a General Conference in 1833, the following is the XVth Section:—

"Concerning imposition of hands, we believe it was the practice of the Apostles and the primitive Church, to lay hands upon the newly baptized believers, and it should be perpetuated in the Church. We therefore practise it. Acts viii. 17; xix. 6; Hebrews vi. 2.—*Rupp's History of Religious Denominations*, p. 81.

(60)

SIX-PRINCIPLE BAPTISTS.

This division of Baptists is spoken of by their historian as of "high antiquity," and having "long maintained their respectability." Their views in reference to *Confirmation* should be noticed in this place. Their distinguishing principles, from which they take their name, are founded on Hebrews vi. 1st and 2d verses. Among them, of course, is the doctrine of the *laying on of hands*. Dr. Belcher, in his history of the "Religious Denominations of the United States," thus speaks of them:

"In this country, however, the chief point on which they have insisted has been that of laying hands on the newly baptized. They refused to hold fellowship with Churches who did not practise this, as they believe, Christian ordinance." "We have intimated the high antiquity of the Six-principle Baptists; and the reader who has examined English Baptist History, must have observed that they were long ago numerous and useful. There seems to have been more of union between them and other Baptists, in their early history, than after-

6

wards. Unhappily, a dispute arose in the
general body on the use of psalmody, against
which the Six-principle Baptists were usually found, and in this dispute one or more
of the most respectable London Churches
originated, though it is highly probable that
their present members know not that either
the Six-principles, or opposition to singing,
had any thing to do with their commence-
ment." (!)

"The same remark may apply to this
country. One of these principles—that of
laying on of hands—was believed, and acted
on for a time by Roger Williams' Church, in
Rhode Island; but these peculiarities among
them soon died away," [*not for one hundred
and sixty-nine years*—see page 68.] "Not
so, however, at Newport, in that State; for,
in 1656, twenty-five members left the first
Church in that town, and formed themselves
into a separate body, on account of the old
Church using psalmody; because it imposed
undue restraints of prophesying, held the
doctrine of particular redemption, and regarded the laying on of hands with indifference. This Church, however, has long ago
changed its views of these things, except
indeed the laying on of hands, which is still
practised. The extent of this branch of the
Baptist body was never large, and according
to the latest statistics they have but seventeen

churches, fifteen ministers, and two thousand one hundred and eighty-nine members."— *Belcher's Religious Denominations*, p. 246.

ENGLISH AND WELSH BAPTISTS.

This attachment to Confirmation is by no means peculiar, however, to these smaller divisions of this denomination. It was once held in great esteem throughout the whole body.

It was recognized as an "Ordinance of Christ" in their confessions, and practised in many of their Churches for more than a hundred years after their first formation. It seems to have grown into disuse by slow degrees, and yet was earnestly advocated and contended for by many of their most learned and influential men. This was the case both in England and America.

The faithful perseverance with which many congregations and associations adhered to this Apostolic rite, which they called one of the doctrines of Christ, referring to Hebrews

vi., 1 and 2, is a very interesting and instructive chapter in their history. It shows us
how remorseless is the innovating hand of
man in matters of religion, and that when
he has once begun to *improve* upon the divine plan, there will be no end short of entire
destruction. For the following statements, in
reference to the English and Welsh Baptists,
we are indebted to Crosby's History of the
English Baptists, a standard work by an ar-
dent admirer of their principles. We copy
from the London edition, of 1740.

The Baptists in Wales were equally at-
tached to this rite with their brethen in England. Among the several biographical notices that this history contains, is one of
Mr. Vavasor Powell, who was a celebrated
preacher in Wales, a man of university education, and belonging to a distinguished
family. He died in 1670, but left a Confession of Faith, which, according to Crosby,
contained not only his own opinions, " but
the faith and discipline of the Churches in
Wales," of which he says: "They were also
for ordination of Elders, singing of Psalms
and Hymns in public worship, *laying on of*

hands on the newly baptized, and anointing the sick with oil, according to the Apostolic direction."—*Crosby*, vol. i. p. 378.

Among these biographical notices is one of Mr. Benjamin Keach, a very prominent preacher in England, and a man of much influence and ability. He exercised his ministry among the Baptists, between the years 1688 and 1704. He was an earnest advocate for *laying on of hands*, and left among his works an elaborate treatise on this subject, entitled "Darkness Vanquished, being an answer to Danvers, on *laying on of hands*." In his biography of this man, Crosby gives the following account of the views of the Baptists of that time concerning this rite.

"This truly famous servant of Christ did not only stand up in defense of believers' baptism, in opposition to that of infants; but also enaged in many controversies that were urged among the Baptists themselves. The first of this kind was about the practice of *laying on of hands upon baptized* persons, and performing it with prayer at their admission in the Church. Those Baptists that held the principles of the Remonstrants *generally practised* it, but those who are called *Calvinists* were divided upon it. *Some*

6*

of *their* Churches did not practise it at all.
Some made it indifferent, and some admitted
members either with or without it. *Others
made it a boundary of their communion, and
would receive none into their societies but by
this method.* And of this last opinion was
Mr. Keach's Church, and they have been tenacious of this opinion even to this day.
These things occasioned several treatises to
be wrote on each side, and it had been con-
troverted among the Baptists ever since
their first forming themselves into distinct
Churches. But as some came from the Established Church, who use it under the name
of *Confirmation*, and others from the Presbyterians and Independents who used it not,
so they brought their different sentiments
in this point along with them. In the Confession of Faith, which was published by
the Baptists in the year 1643, there is no
mention made of it, nor in any other agreed
to afterwards by those of the *Calvinistic* per-
suasion.* But in the declaration of faith
put forth by the English Baptists, who were
fugitives in Holland in the year 1611, they
declare that the elders and deacons are to
be chosen by election and approbation of
that church or congregation whereof they

* This, of course, has no reference to the Philadelphia Confession.

are members, with fasting, prayer, and laying on of hands. And in the declaration
put forth by the Arminian Baptists, about
the year 1660, it is acknowledged *to be the
duty of all baptized believers, and necessary
to a right constituted church.* Their words
are these: ' *That it is the duty of all such,
who are believers baptized, to draw nigh
unto God in submission to that principle of
Christ's doctrine, to wit, prayer and laying
on of hands, that they may receive the promise of the Holy Spirit, whereby they may
mortify the deeds* of the body, and live in
all things answerably to their professed intentions and desires, even to the honor of
him who hath called them out of darkness
into his marvellous light. That it is the
duty of such, who are constituted as afore-
said, to continue steadfastly in Christ's and
the Apostles' doctrine, and assembling together in fellowship, in breaking bread, and
prayers.' The chief advocates for this practice, among the Baptists, were Mr. Samuel
Fisher, Mr. William Rider, Mr. Tomlimson,
Mr. Griffith, Mr. Keach, and Mr. Grantham;
several Baptists on the other side united in
publishing a treatise against it, and especially
against separating about it, entitled, *A
Search for Schism*, but concealed their
names. And Mr. Danvers, who had wrote
so well against infant baptism, set himself

very zealously to the opposing of this practice, and published a treatise on it in the
year 1674.   This, with Mr. Keach's answer,
takes in the sum of the controversy on both
sides, and has so far put an end to it that
scarcely any thing has been published upon
it since."—*Crosby*, vol. iv. p. 291–292.

However, this did not "put an end" to
the *practice*, as Crosby has just above informed us that Mr. Keach's Church was
"tenacious" of it till his own day, which
was more than sixty years after.   It was also
brought to this country, as will be presently
seen, adopted in their first American Confession, and *practised for more than a hundred
and sixty years*, in the first and parent congregation, as well as a long time in many
others.

AMERICAN BAPTISTS.

In the earliest Baptist Congregations established in this country, we find the ordinance of "laying on of hands" prevailing
from the beginning, and also, that the first
"Association" formed set forth in their Con-

fession, their belief that this rite was an "ordinance of Christ to *abide* in the Church." Our authority for the following statements is the "History of the Baptists in America," by David Benedict, Pastor of the Baptist Church in Pawtucket, R. I., Ed. 1813. The first Baptist Church in this country was in Providence, R. I., and was organized by Roger Williams in 1639. In this Congregation, "laying on of hands" seems to have been practised from the beginning; and though, according to our author, it was sometimes "held in a lax manner," it was not laid aside by any order or action of the Church till as late as the year 1808. The fourth Pastor of this Congregation, in succession from Roger Williams, was Thomas Olney, who came to Providence in 1654. Benedict says of him: "He was the chief who made a division about laying on of hands. He and others withdrew, and formed a separate church; but it continued only a short time."—Vol. i. p. 478. We are not informed whether Mr. Olney's separation was because of the "lax manner" in which laying on of hands was held, or whether it was because he refused to recognize it at all. The former, however, is the unavoidable inference. For we soon find the controversy was again revived by another Pastor, who was equally zealous for the traditions of their fathers. A Mr. Samuel Windsor was Pastor of this Congregation, from 1759 to 1770. When, asking for an assistant, the Church appointed the Rev. James Manning, President of the Rhode Island College, with whom Mr. Windsor refused to become associated on account of his lax views concerning laying on of hands,—though it is said of him,—"He himself received it, and administered it to those who desired it." Still Mr. Windsor and his adherents withdrew, and organized a new Congregation, having presented the following declaration to the Church-meeting, signed by himself and a number of members:

" Brethren and Sisters.—We must, in conscience, withdraw ourselves from all those who do not hold strictly to the six principles of the doctrine of Christ, as laid down in Hebrews vi. 1, 2."—Ib. 480.

The subsequent history of this practice is thus recorded by Benedict:

" The doctrine of laying on of hands was, at the beginning of this church, held in a lax manner; but *it became afterward a term of communion*, and continued so till after Dr. Manning came among them: he prevailed with the Church to admit to *occasional* communion, those brethren who were not convinced of the duty of coming under hands; but very few such were received as *members* till after his death. But on August 4, 1791, the Church had a full meeting, when this point was distinctly considered, and a clear vote was gained to admit members who did not hold that doctrine. But notwithstanding this vote, the laying on of hands, not as an ordinance, but as a form of receiving new members, was generally practised until 1808, when the pastor of the Church who had been educated in the belief of this ceremony, as his father was an advocate for it, and who had hitherto practised it, not however without troublesome scruples of its propriety, found his mind brought to a stand on the subject, and after duly weighing the matter, informed the Church that he could no longer continue the practice, and unless they could excuse him, he must ask a dismission from his pastoral care.

After a full discussion of the subject, the Church, with but one dissenting voice, voted *not* to dismiss him; and laying on of hands, of course, fell into neglect.

Some few worthy members were desirous of retaining both their pastor and this ancient ceremony; but not being disposed to act against the voice of the Church, no division, and but little controversy, ensued."— Benedict. vol. i. p. 487.

This is a very significant history, and it shows what a firm hold this doctrine had in the minds of the followers and disciples of Roger Williams, in the first and oldest Baptist Congregation in this country. It took *one hundred and sixty-nine years* to root it completely out!

There are many scraps of history remaining concerning this rite in connection with other congregations and pastors. Mr. Comer was pastor of the Newport congregation in 1726, of whom Benedict says:

"His ministry in this place was short but successful; by his means singing in public was introduced, which had not before been introduced. The laying on of hands was held in a lax manner, and his attempts to urge it as an indispensable duty, though not as a term of communion, gave offense to two leading members in the Church, and was the means of his being dismissed from his office. . . . . Mr. Comer bid fair to be one of the most eminent ministers of his day; his character was unspotted and his talents respectable and popular. He had conceived the design of writing the history of the American Baptists; and for the purpose of forwarding it, traveled as far as Philadelphia— opened a correspondence with persons in the different Colonies, and also in England and Ireland. He was curious in making minutes of remarkable events of every kind:—he also collected many useful facts for his intended history. These minutes, in the few years of his ministry, swelled to two vols. folio, of about sixty pages each—and have been of singular advantage to Edwards, Backus, and the writer of this sketch of this promising man, whom a mysterious providence saw fit to cut down, almost in the beginning of his course."—Ib. 497.

The opinion of such a man would be thought to be of great value. But in his attempt to restore an ancient rite of the Church, he was overruled by "two leading members of his congregation, and dismissed from his office"!

Professor Cutting, of the University of Rochester, in his "Historical Vindications,"

calls him the "young and saintly Comer,"
but overlooks Benedict's statement concerning the cause of his separation from the
Newport congregation, and says, "he re-
tired, in part because some could not bear his
preaching the doctrines of grace"!

The "lax manner" in which the doctrine
of laying on of hands was held in this
Church, led to the forming of a second congregation more than sixty years before Mr.
Comer's effort to restore it to its proper observance. In 1656, "twenty-one persons
broke off from the first Church, and formed
themselves into a separate body." They give
four objections against the old Church, the
last of which is, "her holding the laying on
of hands as a matter of indifference." Benedict adds: "This last article is supposed to
have been the principal cause of separation."
Vol. i. p. 500.

This adherence to the laying on of hands
was not confined to an occasional clergyman
or congregation. In 1729, an Association
or General Convention was held in Rhode
Island, in which thirteen Churches were re-
presented, with ten ministers, two hundred

and fifty communicants, and one thousand auditors. Benedict adds: " *The Churches were all strenuous for the laying on of hands.*"

This Association embraced all the Churches but three· east of New Jersey, and they were the only ones that did not practise laying on of hands. These were the first Churches in Newport, Swansea, and Boston. " It is now, (1813) eighty-four years since this great Association, as it was then esteemed, was held; very considerable changes have taken place in most of the Churches, of which it was then composed; but the same body, on the same plan of doctrine and discipline, still exists under the name of the Rhode Island Yearly Meeting. This meeting, on account of its making the laying on of hands a term of Communion, and its inclination to the Arminian system of doctrine, has no connection with any of the neighboring associations. It contains thirteen Churches, twelve ministers, and over eleven hundred members. Eight of the Churches are in this State, the others in Massachusetts and New York."—*Benedict*, vol. i. p. 508.

In the same author's account of the " Red Stone Association in Western Pennsylvania," he says: " The doctrine of the laying on of hands became a subject of dispute

among the Red Stone Churches a number of
years ago. *Most of them had, from the beginning,* practised the rite, but some were
for making it a term of Communion; it was,
however, finally determined that all should
be left to act according to their respective
opinions on the subject."—Ib., p. 601.

In the Middle States the laying on of
hands seems to have been held in the same
"lax manner," till the subject was revived
by the Churches of Welsh descent. In the
year 1703, a number of Baptists separated
from the Church of Pennepack, in Pennsylvania, and removed to the *Welsh Tract,* in
New Castle county, "on account of a difference about laying on of hands; for the
Church at Pennepack had grown indifferent
about the rite, but *they* deemed it a pre-
requisite to the Communion of Saints." In
1606, a Conference met to arrange the difficulty, who agreed that "a member in either
Church might transiently commune with
the other; that a member who desired to
come under the laying on of hands, might
have his liberty without offense; that the
votaries of the rite might preach or debate
upon the subject with all freedom, consistent

with brotherly love." This arrangement led to the very general observance of the rite, for the account which Benedict gives, taken from the Welsh Tract Church Book, closes thus :—

"From that time forth our brethren held sweet Communion together at the Lord's table, and our minister was invited to preach and assist at an ordination at Pennepack, after the death of brother Watts. He proceeded from thence to the Jerseys, where he enlightened many in the good ways of the Lord, insomuch that in three years after, *all the ministers, and about fifty-five private members had submitted to the ordinance.*" To this account Benedict adds the following :—

"The Welsh Tract Church was the principal, if not the sole means of introducing singing, *imposition of hands*, Church covenants, etc., among the Baptists of the Middle States. The *Century Confession* was in America before the year 1716, but without the articles which relate to these subjects; that year they were inserted by the Rev. Abel Morgan, who translated the Confession to Welsh, about which time it was signed by one hundred and twenty-two members of this Church. These articles were inserted in the next English edition, and adopted with the other articles by the Philadelphia Association, in 1742."—*Benedict*, vol. ii. p. 6.

This practice prevailed in other parts of the United States, as well as in these thus noticed; and there is no reason for doubting that wherever the Baptists of that day went, they carried with them their attachment to this rite. It was so in Tennessee and Virginia, according to the same author we have already so often quoted. An Association in the latter State held to nine Christian rites, among which laying on of hands was one. And while many of these, after a time, fell into disuse, Benedict says of this: "The Ordinance, as they esteem it, of laying on of hands, and the office of ruling Elders, they still retain."—Vol. ii. p. 108.

It must appear from these quotations, that the laying on of hands was of very general prevalence among the first Baptists in this country. But over and above this practice, we have their declaration in favor of the rite in their first confession. This was set forth by the Philadelphia Association, in September, 1742. The 35th Chapter of this Confession is headed, "Of Laying on of Hands," and is as follows:—

"We believe that laying on of hands, with prayer, upon baptized believers, as such, is *an ordinance of Christ*, and ought to be submitted unto by all such persons as are admitted to partake of the Lord's Supper, and that the end of this ordinance is not for the extraordinary gifts of the Spirit, but for the farther reception of the Holy Spirit of promise, or for the addition of the graces of the Spirit, and the influences thereof; to confirm, strengthen, and comfort them in Christ Jesus; it being ratified and established by the extraordinary gifts of the Spirit *in the primitive times, to abide in the Church*, as meeting together on the first day of the week was, that being the day of worship or Christian Sabbath, under the gospel; and as preaching the word was, and as baptism was, and prayer was, and singing psalms, etc., was, so this laying on of hands was; for as the whole gospel was confirmed by signs and wonders, and divers miracles of the Holy Ghost in general, so was every ordinance in like manner confirmed in particular." The texts of Scripture referred to, to substantiate this Article, are, Hebrews vi. 1, 2; Acts viii. 17, 18; xix. 6; Eph. i. 13, 14, etc.

To this Confession of Faith there was at

the same time added a Treatise of Discipline, which gives the following directions concerning the manner in which new members are to be received into Church communion, after having given a satisfactory account of their faith and experience:

"And after the person is baptized according to the institution and command of Christ, *and come under the imposition of hands of the Elders of the Church, according to the practice of the Apostles,* the Pastor, Minister, or Elders, as presiding in the acts of the Church's power, do receive such an one into the communion and fellowship of that Church in particular."

I am indebted for these extracts from this Confession to a *reprint* in a recent work by Professor Cutting, of the Rochester University, called "Historical Vindications." How this Confession was received and regarded by the Baptists generally, we can best learn by reference to their own authorities. Professor Cutting, in the work just referred to, says:

"The cordial reception and the authoritative character of the creed statements embraced in the Confession, are beyond question. From a period a little later than this, to the end of the century, nearly every year a chapter of the Confession was made the subject of a Pastoral Address to the Churches. This venerable formulary never, indeed, usurped the place of the Word of God; but *distinctly, cordially*, and always, it was a declaration to the world of the doctrines which the Association regarded as taught in the Bible." Historical Vindications, p. 96.

Again: The Minutes of this *Association* were republished in Philadelphia in 1851 by a Committee consisting of Horatio Jones, D.D., Howard Malcom, D.D., Rev. A. D. Gillette, Wilson Jewell, Joseph Taylor, and Wm. Shadrack. The Preface of these Minutes says of this Confession of 1742:

"It is in substance the same as that of the Ancient Baptists in Poland and Bohemia; and of the Mennonists in Holland, and the early English and Welsh Churches. This Confession was published by Ministers and brethren, representing about forty Churches, met in London in 1689. It was printed for the Philadelphia Association by Benjamin Franklin, and numerous editions have since been issued. *Throughout the United States, it is generally considered the Standard of orthodoxy among Baptists.*"

The same difficulty, however, was soon ex-
perienced in the *Association* that we have
seen in the various Congregations, in holding fast to this primitive rite. Without the
creeds, the Ministry, and the Liturgy of
Apostolic times, *this* primitive ordinance
could not long be retained. And so we find
indications of lax views prevailing in the
Association in reference to the obligation of
Confirmation as early as 1783. The Association of this year answers a query from the
Newtown Church in reference to this matter,
as follows:

"We observe that imposition of hands on
baptized persons has been the general practice of the Churches in union with this Association, *and is still used by most of them*, but
it was never considered by the Association
as a bar of Communion. Resolved, that any
person scrupling to submit thereto, may be
admitted to the fellowship of the Church
without it." *Minutes*, p. 194.

So hard is it to hold fast to one "*ordinance
of Christ*" without all his institutions in their
integrity! In 1742, this was declared to be
"an ordinance of Christ, which ought to be

submitted unto by all such persons as are admitted to partake of the Lord's Supper;" and only forty years have passed, when it is given up to the "scrupling" of any one!

MR. WESLEY.

THAT Mr. Wesley was in favor of *Confirmation* there can be little doubt, when we remember how often and how emphatically he commends the "religion of the Church of England" to his followers. In the preface to the "Methodist Prayer Book," which Mr. Wesley issued in 1784, is the following testimony to the excellency of the Liturgy of the Church of England:

"I believe there is no Liturgy in the world, either in any ancient or modern language, which breathes more of a solid, scriptural, rational piety than the Common Prayer of the Church of England. And though the main of it was compiled more than two hundred years ago, yet is the language of it not only pure, but strong and elegant in the highest degree. Little alteration is made in

(84)

the following edition of it, which I recom-
mend to our Societies in America." *Preface
to the "Sunday Services of the Methodists in
North America."*

It would be easy to quote *many* such
general commendations of the doctrines and
practices of the Church of England, in which
Mr. Wesley was born, and in which he died.
Thus, his Sermons contain many such sentiments as these:

"Methodism, so called, is the old religion,
the religion of the Bible, the religion of the
Primitive Church, the religion of the Church
of England."—Vol. ii. p. 493. "Whenever
the Methodists leave the Church, God will leave
them."—Ib., p. 497. "We do not—will not
—form any separate sect, but, from *principle*,
remain what we always have been, true members of the Church of England."—p. 498.

And so in his sermon on the Ministerial
Office.—Vol. ii. p. 542. Mr. Wesley says:
"*I hold all the doctrines of the Church of England. I love her liturgy—I approve her plan
of discipline, and only wish it could be put in
execution.*" As *Confirmation* is so very prominent in the discipline of the Church of
England, it must have been in Mr. Wesley's
mind when he made this statement.

In his "Notes on the New Testament,"
8

under Hebrews vi. 1., he says—"And when they believed they were baptized with the baptism (not of the Jews or John), but of Christ. The next thing was to lay hands upon them, that they might receive the Holy Ghost, after which they were fully instructed touching the resurrection and the general judgment."

It is manifest that Mr. Wesley is setting forth that exposition of *the principles of the doctrines of Christ*, which he regards as binding upon men now—among which principles is the laying on of hands upon Christians that they may receive the Holy Ghost.

The practice of the first Methodists was in conformity with these views, they went to the Church for baptism and the Lord's Supper, and for Confirmation also. Of this practice the case of Dr. Adam Clarke, given below, is an instance.

ADAM CLARKE.

DR. ADAM CLARKE is known to have been a man of great piety, and one of the most learned

divines ever numbered among the Methodists.
His writings are deservedly held in great
esteem by both the ministers and people of
this large body. Scattered throughout them
there are to be found many statements en-
dorsing and commending what are thought
to be the peculiar doctrines of the Church
of England, and giving also the highest
praise to the learning, piety, and devotion of
her Bishops and Clergy. Thus he says of
the Prayer Book:

"*Next to the Bible, it is the book of my un-
derstanding and of my heart.*"

Again he says:

"I was born so to speak in the Church;
baptized in the Church; brought up in it;
confirmed in it, by that most apostolic man,
Dr. Bagot, Bishop of Bristol; *have all my
life held uninterrupted communion with it;
conscientiously believe its doctrines, and have
spoken and written in defense of it.* Being bred
up in its bosom, I early drank in *its salutary
doctrines and spirit.*"—*Life of A. Clarke*, vol. iii.
pp. 110, 111, *Conference Office, N. Y.*

Again he says in his notes on 1 Timothy
iii. 13.

"*Deacon, Presbyter, and Bishop existed in
the Apostolic Church, and therefore may be con-*

sidered of Divine authority." And under the first verse of the same chapter, he says: "In former times Bishops wrote much and preached much, and their labors were greatly owned of God. No Church, since the Apostles' days, has been more honored in this way than the British Church. And although Bishops are *here,* as elsewhere, appointed by the State: yet we cannot help adoring the good providence of God, that, taken as a body, they have been an honor to their function. And since the reformation of religion in these lands, the Bishops have been, in general, men of great learning and probity; and the ablest advocates of the Christian system, both as to its authenticity, and the purity and excellence of its doctrines and morality."

And so he says again, under Acts i. 20:—

"Bishop, is a Scriptural and sacred title, was gloriously supported in the primitive Church, and many to the present day are no less ornaments to the title, than the title is ornamental to them. *The best defenses of the truth of God,* and the Protestant faith are in the works of the Bishops of the British Churches."

On the subject of *Confirmation* we have

from this same distinguished Methodist very full and interesting testimony.

In the first volume of his life, published by the Methodist Book Concern at New York in 1833, he gives the following account of his own Confirmation:

"It was at this time that the Bishop of Bristol held a *Confirmation* in the Collegiate Church. I had never been confirmed, and as I had a high respect for all the rites and ceremonies of the Church, I wished to embrace this opportunity to get the blessing of that amiable and apostolic-looking prelate, Dr. Lewis Bagot. I asked permission: several of the preachers' sons went with me, and I felt much satisfaction in this ordinance: to me it was very solemn, and the whole was well conducted. Mr. S., who was a Presbyterian, pitied my being so 'long held in the oldness of the letter.' I have lived *nearly forty years since*, and upon this point my sentiments are not changed."—*Life of Adam Clarke*, vol. i. p. 94.

Again, in the third volume of the same work is the following letter written by Dr. Clarke only two years before his death:

"DEAR MRS. WILKINSON:—You wish for my opinion on the subject of Confirmation.

8*

It is supposed to be a rite by which the
moral burden is taken off the shoulders of
the sponsors, and transferred to those shoulders to which it properly belongs. Now, as
long as these opinions and feelings prevail
in the minds of all parties, I say, in God's
name, let the rite, duly administered, be hum-
bly received; but the subjects of it should
be well-informed, that by it they have not
merely performed a duty, and so far may
have an easy conscience, but in addition they have by it taken a strong and
perpetual *yoke* upon their necks, in their
vow 'to renounce the Devil and all his
works, the pomps and vanities of this wicked
world, and all the sinful lusts of the flesh,
and that they should keep God's holy will
and commandments, and walk in the same
all the days of their lives.' This is no ordinary obligation. This they solemnly take
on themselves when they come to be confirmed, and by the act they come under a
new and perpetual covenant, to give themselves wholly to God, that they may have a
thorough 'death unto sin,' and a complete
'new birth unto righteousness.' Should any
young person say, 'if all this is comprised in
being confirmed, then I will not be confirmed at all.' I answer, you are bound to
all this by your profession of Christianity.
So that, confirmed or not confirmed, this

yoke is about your neck, and if you break
it, or throw it away, it is at the peril of your
final destruction.

Again the rite itself is useful to call
these things to remembrance, and who knows
how much grace may be received during
the performance of the ceremony, and especially by having a holy man's hands laid
on your head, and the blessing and protec-
tion of God solemnly invoked in your be-
half? Tell these things to your dear daugh-
ters and sons, and tell them another thing
of which few would think—namely, that not
having had the opportunity of being confirmed when I had arrived at that age at
which I had an ecclesiastical right to receive
it, I was determined not to be without it,
and therefore went and *received Confirmation
even since I became a Methodist preacher.* Yes,
I was confirmed in the Collegiate Church,
at Bristol, in the year 1782, by that very
holy man, Dr. Lewis Bagot, then Bishop of that
see, and afterward Bishop of Norwich. You
see now, my good sister, both from my
teaching and from my practice, what I think
of the rite of Confirmation, and I will just
add one word more. I believe the rite will
be very solemnly administered by the Bishop
of London, who will go through the whole
with an honest conscience before God. I
have sometimes thought I should write a

little tract on this, as I did on the third Collect for grace, now called 'The Traveler's Prayer.'—ADAM CLARKE."—*Life of Adam Clarke*, vol. iii. p. 123.

DR. BANGS.

DR. BANGS, a very prominent Methodist preacher in this country, wrote a work called "*An Original Church of Christ*," in which he says of Confirmation:

"That this apostolic practice was and should be continued in the Church is not doubted. Indeed I consider Baptism but half performed unless the application of water to the body is followed by the *imposition of hands and prayer*, that the blessings of the Holy Spirit may descend upon the subjects of this holy ordinance."—*Original Church*, p. 322.

CONCLUSION.

WITH a little more time given to the subject, it would be quite possible to add many
more *admissions* of the same kind, and from
the same sources as those given above.
These, however, are amply sufficient for the
purpose in view, and have already made a
little book of what was at first intended to
be but a little *tract.* The testimony thus
given in favor of the rite of Confirmation, is
from those who, for learning and piety, were,
without question, the most distinguished
men in these various religious denominations. Their knowledge of Scripture and
of the early history of Christianity, left no
room to question the apostolic origin of this
ordinance; and their experience in the Christian Ministry brought the conviction that,
while it was of this inspired authority, it
was also of the highest practical importance
in the Christian Scheme.

The testimony thus given establishes these

three points.—*That the rite of Confirmation was instituted by the inspired Apostles of Jesus Christ, to be of perpetual duration in the Church. That it was universally practised for the first fifteen hundred years. That it is still of great practical utility, and that no modern expedient will serve its place and purpose.* When we remember the ability these men possessed for investigating this subject, and that their prejudices would *naturally* lead them to a different conclusion, such testimony would seem, to a candid and truth-loving mind, an " end of controversy."

In the extracts given from the writings of these distinguished divines there are incidental principles of great interest and importance, which it would be well to notice particularly, if our space allowed.

The deference paid to the authority of the Primitive and Apostolic Church, the weight given to the *historic* testimony of the early days of Christianity, and the *taking for granted* that the Fathers were competent and credible witnesses concerning the doctrines and customs of their own times, should be particularly noticed by those of the present day who have so little reverence for the past. There was evidently no notion, in the minds of these distinguished divines and scholars, of a *new Church*, or of *new doctrines and new rites and customs.*

The compiler has been perhaps more interested in the history of this rite among the Baptists than in any other denomination. It is certainly a very instructive history, and has its lesson of warning to all Christian people. That lesson is,—that the *Church of God* which has been ordained for the preservation and perpetuation of his Word and Ordinances, must be kept and guarded in its *integrity*, or we shall lose one after another of the most precious and vital of its truths. If Episcopacy, and the Creeds, and the Liturgy of the primitive Church had been retained, then Confirmation could easily have been retained also; but when any one of these great anchorages of the Faith is abandoned, no one can tell whither the vessel which bears the precious trust may drift, or upon what shoal or rock it may wreck.